Best Selling Series
CONSOLIDATION EXERCISES
PHOTOCOPIABLE MASTERS

Level 2

Spelling Made

Consolidation Exercises For Spelling Made Easy
Level 2 Text Book

---

by
Violet Brand and Katy Brand

Fun with Phonics
Consolidation Exercises
for
Spelling Made Easy Level 2
First published in the United Kingdom in 2005
by Violet and Katy Brand

Copyright assigned to BrandBooks
(a division of G & M Brand Publications Ltd) Violet Brand and Katy Brand (2005)

ISBN 1-904421-164

All rights reserved. The copymasters contained in this publication are protected by international copyright laws. The copyright of all materials in the 'Spelling Made Easy' series remains the property of the publisher and the authors. The publisher hereby grants photocopying rights of this work for use with 'Spelling Made Easy' textbooks. Otherwise, no part of this book may be reproduced or translated in any form or by any means, electronic or mechanical, including recording or by any information storage or retrieval system without permission in writing from the publisher.

Illustrated by Adam Pickering

CONTENTS
Fun with Phonics
Level 2

Introduction

	Exercises	page	Answers page
1.	Short vowel sounds a, o, i	2,3	54
2.	Short vowel sounds a, o, i	4,5	55
3.	Short Vowel Sounds e, u	6,7	56
4.	Short Vowel Sounds e, u	8,9	57
5.	Consonant Clusters and Phonemes ck, ee, oo	10,11	58
6.	Consonant Clusters and Phonemes ck, ee, oo	12,13	59
7.	Consonant Clusters and Phonemes ar, sh	14,15	60
8.	Consonant Clusters and Phonemes ar, sh	16,17	61
9.	Consonant Clusters and Vowel Blending ch, th, or	18,19	62
10.	Consonant Clusters and Vowel Blending ch, th, or	20,21	63
11.	Magic 'e' 1 a-e, i-e	22,23	64
12.	Magic 'e' 1 a-e, i-e	24,25	65
13.	Magic 'e' 2 o-e, u-e	26,27	66
14.	Magic 'e' 2 o-e, u-e	28,29	67
15.	Vowel Blending ai, oa, ir	30,31	68
16.	Vowel Blending ai, oa, ir	32,33	69

(Cont.)

Contents (continued)

Exercises	page	Answers page
17. Vowel Blending ou, ea, ur	34, 35	70
18. Vowel Blending ou, ea, ur	36, 37	71
19. Vowel Blending aw, oi, er	38, 39	72
20. Vowel Blending aw, oi, er	40, 41	73
21. Vowel Blending al, ea (short e), ow	42, 43	74
22. Vowel Blending al, ea (short e), ow	44, 45	75
23. Silent Letters a (ar) and Endings	46, 47	76
24. Silent Letters a (ar) and Endings	48, 49	77
25. Various	50, 51	78
26. Various	52, 53	79

INTRODUCTION

BrandBooks is delighted to bring you Fun With Phonics, a series of consolidation exercises to perfectly complement the rest of Violet Brand's best-selling Spelling Made Easy series. Fun With Phonics comprises a set of four workbooks, colour-coded to match each of the existing textbooks and worksheet books.

Each Fun With Phonics book is fully photocopiable and designed to be used in conjunction with its corresponding textbook. Each book takes between two and five of the word families found in the textbook and provides four pages of interesting and stimulating exercises, including passages for reading aloud, reading comprehension tests, word searches, crosswords and much more.

Each series of exercises is based on a continuous story featuring Gus, the well-known character from the textbooks. In many cases pupils will not recognise that they are being tested and that basic skills are being reinforced. Field tests have shown that pupils simply enjoy them. They are designed to put the fun into phonics!

The Spelling Made Easy series was conceived, written and published at a time when teaching reading and spelling though phonics was out of fashion in the UK, as were multi-sensory techniques.

After publication in 1984 the textbook series was quickly recognised as highly effective and it continues to be widely used and purchased by primary and special schools in the UK and their equivalents in other parts of the world where English is taught.

Violet Brand was awarded the MBE for services to literacy, and has always believed that literacy skills must be taught in a way that is both relevant and fun in order to become a tool for life.

"Spelling in isolation is not enough. The word building skills acquired must be integrated into literacy generally. For a few children this will happen automatically, but for others, tasks which will gently edge them along the path will be essential. Constant reinforcement will be necessary."

– Violet Brand MBE

1. Short Vowel Sounds
'a', 'o', 'i'

Spelling Made Easy
Level 2 Textbook
Pages 6 - 11

1a Reading Exercise

Gus is a tramp with no family and no home. He has a dog and a pet badger. It is easy to distrust Gus, or dismiss him as a misfit. But Gus is a good man. He can be difficult to find as he drifts from place to place, but he is content. He never gets cross or bossy. Gus is standing on a bridge on the canal when a jogger spots him. The jogger stops in his tracks. He thinks he remembers Gus's face. He has not made a mistake. The jogger runs to the bridge. He wants to get a better look.

1b Reading Comprehension

Use the story to answer the following questions:

1. Gus has a pet dog. He has another pet. What is it?

2. Who spots Gus?

3. Where is Gus standing when he is spotted?

4. How does Gus get from place to place?

5. Where does the jogger stop?

6. Gus never gets cross or _____.

1c Pictures

Write the correct word underneath each picture.

1d Wordsearch

There are 10 words from the story hidden in the box below. They only go from left to right.

t	r	a	m	p	h	j	e	r	v
s	x	q	f	y	n	o	t	h	l
r	d	i	s	t	r	u	s	t	b
f	o	t	e	c	v	m	a	n	z
s	p	o	t	s	g	x	z	q	k
w	y	u	c	o	n	t	e	n	t
d	m	i	s	f	i	t	j	a	e
u	f	a	e	f	a	m	i	l	y
c	r	o	s	s	t	x	y	o	v
q	o	g	d	i	s	m	i	s	s

1e Wordmuddle

Write the words below next to the correct heading. Some of the words do not appear in the story.

      knock   mistake   angry

      drifts   tracks   bossy

a _____   _____

o _____   _____

i _____   _____

1f Choose your favourite sentence from the story. On a separate sheet of paper, draw a picture of the sentence. Write the sentence next to your picture, then colour in the picture.

2. Short Vowel Sounds
'a', 'o', 'i'

**Spelling Made Easy
Level 2 Textbook
Pages 6 - 11**

2a Reading Exercise

The jogger tells Gus he remembers his face. Gus thinks the jogger must be mad. He tells the jogger that he has no family and that he has lost contact with his friends. The jogger tells Gus his name is Adam. He thinks that perhaps the two men met at a disco or a rugby match. Gus says he has never been to a disco, but he did go to a rugby match when he was twenty years old. Gus takes off his cap to scratch his head. 'This is mad!' he thinks. He has to admit that he feels knocked out. Adam offers to get Gus a cup of tea in the shop. Gus does not want to dismiss Adam.

2b Reading Comprehension

Use the story to answer the following questions:

1. What is the jogger's name?

2. What has Gus lost with his friends?

3. Where is the first place Adam thinks he met Gus?

4. How does Gus feel?

5. Where do they go for tea?

6. What does Gus not want to do with Adam?

2c Picture   There are 3 words from the story in the picture below. Write the correct words underneath the box.

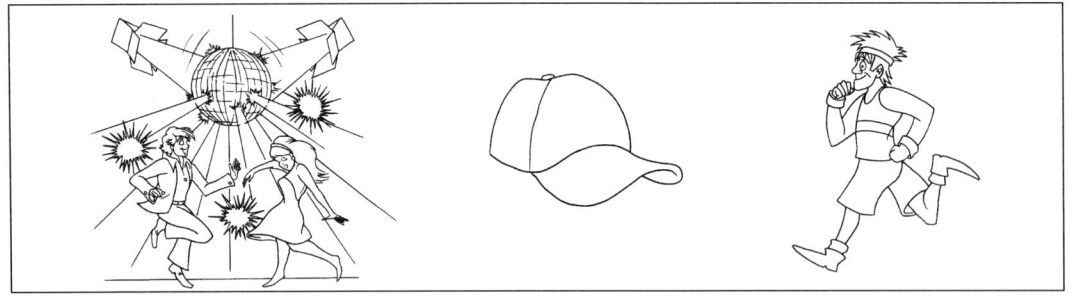

_____   _____   _____

2d Crossword

Use the clues and the story to fill in the boxes.

Across
1. To say you made a mistake. (5)
2. He runs for fun. (6)
3. A kind of hat. (3)
4. You feel calm and happy. (7)
5. A sports meeting. (5)

Down
1. A place to have a dance. (5)
2. Do this to make an itch go away. (7)
3. To rap on the door. (5)

2e Wordsorting

Below are 6 new words. Write them next to the correct heading.

attack   glossy   minimum

prompt   wrist   plastic

a _____   _____

o _____   _____

i _____   _____

2f On a separate sheet of paper draw a picture of EITHER a rugby match OR a disco. Label the picture and colour it in.

3. Short Vowel Sounds
'e', 'u'

**Spelling Made Easy
Level 2 Textbook
Pages 12 - 15**

3a Reading Exercise

Adam and Gus go to the teashop. Gus does not like the public as they look at him with disgust. He is a tramp so people distrust and judge him, but not Adam. Gus likes Adam but he does not know what to expect – it all seems very odd! The teashop is hectic. There are seventeen people inside who want drinks and snacks. Adam and Gus sit close to the exit. Adam has milk and Gus has tea. There is a sudden shout from the back of the teashop. A hundred pounds is missing from the electric till. All the people in the shop suspect that Gus is the culprit. They want to expel him from the shop. Adam thinks this is very unjust.

3b Reading Comprehension

Use the story to answer the following questions:

1. Why doesn't Gus like the public?
2. What two things do people do because Gus is a tramp?
3. What word is used in the story to describe the teashop?
4. How many people are in the teashop?
5. What do Adam and Gus sit close to?
6. What does Adam think about the people suspecting Gus?

3c Pictures – use the story and the pictures to fill in the gaps.

The teashop is _____.

There is a _____ shout.

A _____ pounds is missing.

People want to _____ Gus from the teashop.

3d Wordsearch

There are 8 words from the story hidden in the box below. They go from left to right and top to bottom.

o	p	r	t	d	v	b	n	d	e
c	u	s	z	x	q	p	f	d	l
u	b	s	u	d	d	e	n	c	e
l	l	k	g	h	m	y	r	f	c
p	i	d	i	s	t	r	u	s	t
r	c	v	b	g	d	s	e	h	r
i	x	s	u	s	p	e	c	t	i
t	f	c	o	z	r	y	u	j	c
z	w	r	u	e	x	p	e	l	k
e	x	p	e	c	t	o	l	v	b

3e Wordmuddle

Write the words below next to the correct heading. Some of the words do not appear in the story.

    culprit   seven   unpack

    hedge   struck   electric

e _____ _____ _____

u _____ _____ _____

3f On a separate sheet of paper, draw a picture of the teashop then colour it in.

4. Short Vowel Sounds
'e', 'u'

Spelling Made Easy
Level 2 Textbook
Pages 12 - 15

4a Reading Exercise

Everyone in the shop is cross. Gus feels unwell. He wishes he had never met Adam! Adam insists to the man who runs the teashop that there has been a mistake. They unplug the electric till and empty all the cash onto a ledge. Gus tries to tell Adam that people always judge him like this and he expects it, but Adam is disgusted. The man who runs the shop counts up the cash from the till. It is all there so a mistake has been made. Gus and Adam get their drinks for free but they make a swift exit. Gus is glad that Adam stuck up for him. He was not expecting it from someone he had just met.

4b Reading Comprehension

Use the story to answer the following questions:

1. How does Gus feel?

2. What does the man do to the electric till?

3. Where do they empty the cash?

4. How does Adam feel about people judging Gus?

5. What did Adam do to make Gus feel glad?

6. Why was Gus not expecting Adam to stick up for him?

4c Pictures – draw pictures of the words that appear underneath each box.

electric till	plug	a disgusted face

4d Crossword

Use the clues and the story to fill in the boxes.

Across
1. To remove a cable from a socket. (6)
2. The way out. (4)
3. Not powered by a battery. (8)

Down
1. You feel sick. (6)
2. A shelf. (5)
3. The most important person in court. (5)
4. Not full. (5)

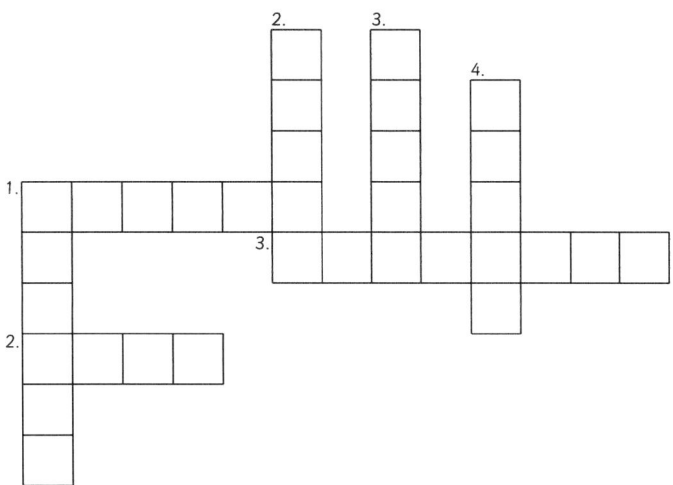

4e Wordsorting

Below are 6 new words. Write them next to the correct heading.

skull   second   umbrella

smell   until   exist

e _____   _____   _____

u _____   _____   _____

4f On a separate sheet of paper, draw a picture of Adam and Gus making a swift exit from the teashop. Colour it in then write a sentence to describe what is happening in the picture.

5. Consonant Clusters and Phonemes
'ck', 'ee', 'oo'

**Spelling Made Easy
Level 2 Textbook
Pages 16 - 21**

5a Reading Exercise

Gus feels very gloomy. Adam gives his hand a squeeze and tells Gus that the man from the shop is a fool. It is noon and the two men are hungry. Gus will not go to another shop, so Adam says they will go back to his house for some food. They go along the embankment next to the canal. A family of ducks swims along. There are two ducks and six ducklings. Gus feels his mood lift. He puts his hand in his pocket for some sweets to feed to the ducks. The ducks swoop on the sweets and Gus smiles. Adam sees Gus's crooked tooth and claps his hands. 'It was you at the rugby match!' he shouts. 'I remember your crooked tooth!'

5b Reading Comprehension

Use the story to answer the questions:

1. How does Gus feel at the beginning of the story?

2. What does Adam do to Gus's hand?

3. What is swimming on the canal?

4. What does Gus feed to the ducks?

5. Where does Gus keep his sweets?

6. What is special about Gus's tooth?

5c Pictures

Write the correct word underneath each picture

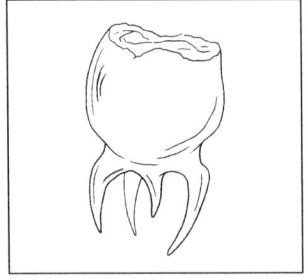

5d Wordsearch

There are 10 words from the story hidden in the box below. They only go from left to right.

t	y	r	s	c	b	f	o	o	d
h	n	o	o	n	g	j	f	s	r
v	b	s	w	e	e	t	s	x	z
w	g	r	y	d	s	b	a	c	k
d	u	c	k	s	u	i	f	d	s
g	t	e	f	o	o	l	p	g	s
c	x	f	e	e	l	s	w	d	f
e	g	d	s	f	o	o	h	c	d
s	e	e	s	z	x	m	o	o	d
p	o	c	k	e	t	w	q	h	r

5e Wordmuddle

Write the words below next to the correct heading. Some of the words do not appear in the story.

swoop   balloon   squeeze

trickle   duckling   free

ck _____   _____

ee _____   _____

oo _____   _____

5f On a separate sheet of paper draw a picture of two ducks and six ducklings swimming on the canal and eating sweets. Colour in your picture then write a sentence to describe what is happening.

6. Consonant Clusters and Phonemes 'ck', 'ee', 'oo'

Spelling Made Easy
Level 2 Textbook
Pages 16 - 21

6a Reading Exercise

Gus and Adam get to Adam's house. Adam lets them in and begins to cook some lunch. He puts out a packet of ham, pickle, cheese and a big jug of orange juice. Adam thinks that Gus's crooked tooth is proof that they have met before. Gus only wants to have some ham and cheese. Gus is not greedy, but he is very hungry! Adam wants to discuss the rugby match. Gus is not really in the mood. He has a sore neck and back. He just wants to sit down! The rugby match was twenty years ago, and that was before Gus was a tramp. Gus is not a sad man, but thinking about the past makes him feel gloomy. He takes out a packet of tissues from his jacket pocket.

6b Reading Comprehension

Use the story to answer the questions:

1. What does Adam begin to do when they get back to the house?

2. Adam puts out ham, cheese and a jug of juice. What is missing?

3. Gus is hungry, but he is not _____.

4. Gus wants to eat ham, and what else?

5. Where does Gus keep his tissues?

6. How does Gus feel when he thinks about the past?

6c Picture – there are 3 words from the story in the picture below. Write the correct words underneath the box.

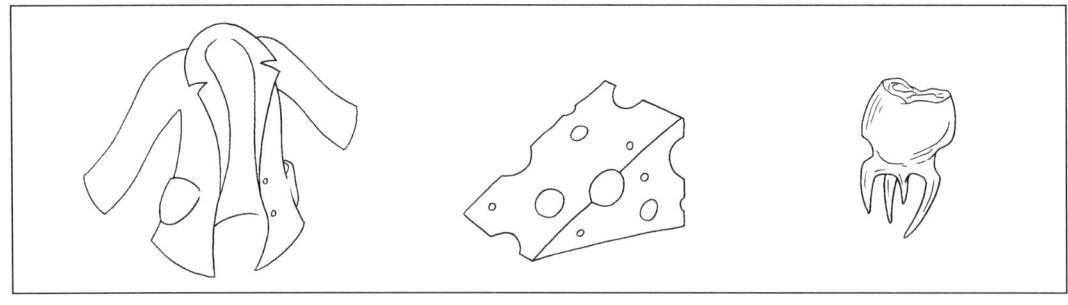

_____   _____   _____

6d Crossword

Use the clues and the story to fill in the boxes.

Across
1. A smart coat. (6)
2. You can do this to an onion. (6)
3. You feel a bit sad. (6)
4. A bit wonky (7)
5. Between your head and shoulders (4)

Down
1. Keep things in this when walking around. (6)
2. You are this if you eat too much. (6)
3. It may be cheddar or edam. (6)

6e Wordsorting

Below are 6 new words. Write them next to the correct heading.

ticket   scoop   smack

sleeve   knee   choose

ck _____   _____

ee _____   _____

oo _____   _____

6f Choose your three favourite types of food. On a separate sheet of paper, draw a picture of them and also some cheese, a packet of ham and some pickle. Colour in the picture then label each item.

7. Consonant Clusters and Phonemes 'ar', 'sh'

**Spelling Made Easy
Level 2 Textbook
Pages 22 - 25**

7a Reading Exercise

Gus has a think. He starts to shake. He starts to shudder and shake his head. Adam tells Gus it is just a story so it can do no harm. In a flash, Gus sees that he is being selfish, so he agrees to tell Adam about the rugby match. Gus says that twenty years ago he was an artist.
He would sell his cartoons in the market. He had lots of friends and lots of cash. He was happy. Then he went to the rugby match for fun.
He took his car and on his way home he had a crash. He broke his arm in the crash and so he could not be an artist anymore. His life as an artist was finished. He lost his job, his money and his market stand.
He became a tramp.

7b Reading Comprehension

Use the story to answer the questions:

1. What does Gus start to do when he has a think?

2. What does Adam say about the story?

3. What does Gus see in a flash?

4. Where did Gus sell his cartoons?

5. What happened to Gus's car?

6. What did Gus break in the crash?

7c Pictures – use the story and the pictures to fill in the gaps.

Gus starts to _____ and _____ his head.

Gus would sell his cartoons at the _____.

Gus had lots of friends and lots of _____.

Gus had a crash in his _____ and broke his _____.

7d Wordsearch

There are 8 words from the story hidden in the box below. They go from left to right and top to bottom.

c	d	f	g	w	x	a	c	f	j
a	k	l	f	s	v	r	b	m	s
s	s	h	a	k	e	t	c	a	r
h	u	q	w	x	s	i	z	v	b
t	y	d	s	h	j	s	k	m	d
x	h	a	r	m	w	t	d	o	r
j	f	x	m	a	r	k	e	t	w
s	e	l	f	i	s	h	m	c	e
v	h	s	r	o	f	e	t	x	a
r	t	s	x	f	l	a	s	h	b

7e Wordmuddle

Write the words below next to the correct heading. Some of the words do not appear in the story.

        harm   mash   selfish

        punish   alarm   carpet

ar _____ _____ _____

sh _____ _____ _____

7f On a separate sheet of paper draw a cartoon of yourself standing with Gus and Adam, then colour it in using bold, bright colours!

8. Consonant Clusters and Phonemes   **Spelling Made Easy**
    'ar', 'sh'   **Level 2 Textbook**
                                                                Pages 22 - 25

8a Reading Exercise

Adam is shocked and sad for Gus. Gus tells Adam not to be alarmed. He is happy now. Gus shows Adam his scar from the crash. It runs up his left arm. Apart from the scar, he was unharmed, and Gus was thankful for that. Gus tells Adam he does not remember him. Adam tells Gus he was just ten years old at the time. He tells Gus that he got lost and that Gus helped him find his parents. Gus smiles. It is getting dark. Adam's wife will be home soon. She will cook some shrimps, mash and parsnips for supper. Gus feels happy to have finished the story of his past. He thinks about being an artist. He would like to make a cartoon of Adam.

8b Reading Comprehension

Use the story to answer the questions:

1. What two emotions does Adam feel when he hears Gus's story?

2. What does Gus tell Adam not to be?

3. What does Gus have on his left arm?

4. What three things will Adam's wife cook for supper?

5. What would Gus like to make for Adam?

8c Pictures – draw pictures of the words that appear underneath each box.

parsnip	arm	a shocked face

8d Crossword

Use the clues and the story to fill in the boxes.

Across
1. A type of drawing that is often funny. (7)
2. You feel this if you get a bad surprise. (7)
3. Do this to potatoes. (4)
4. A person who paints pictures (6)

Down
1. Two cars driving into each other. (5)
2. A type of sea creature. (6)
3. The mark left by a cut. (4)

8e Wordsorting

Below are 6 new words. Write them next to the correct heading.

shaking   dark   splash

department   snarl   finish

ar _____   _____   _____

sh _____   _____   _____

8f On a separate sheet of paper, draw a picture of a big plate of shrimps, mash and parsnips. Add a bowl of your favourite pudding. Colour in your picture then label all the different items.

9. Consonant Clusters and Vowel Blending
'ch', 'th', 'or'

**Spelling Made Easy
Level 2 Textbook
Pages 26 – 31**

9a Reading Exercise

Adam and Gus are thirsty. They need a drink to wet their throats. Adam makes some tea and offers Gus some cherries. Adam tells Gus he has three children. Two of them are away on a trip and the third is staying with his Gran. Adam says that his children are very important to him. One child has been to see the doctor. They were playing next to the canal and one fell in. They threw him a rope and got him to the shore. He had broken his thumb but apart from that he was OK. Adam then made a change to the rules. It is now forbidden for the children to play by the canal without him.

9b Reading Comprehension

Use the story to answer the questions:

1. Why do Adam and Gus need a drink?
2. What does Adam offer Gus to go with his tea?
3. How many children does Adam have?
4. Who did one of Adam's children have to see about his thumb?
5. What did Adam do with the rope?
6. What did Adam change about the rules?

9c Pictures

Write the correct word underneath each picture.

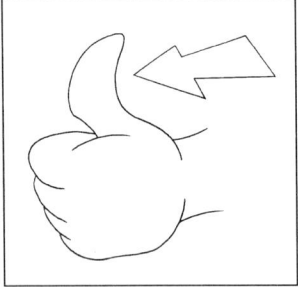

9d Wordsearch

There are 10 words from the story hidden in the box below. They only go from left to right.

i	m	p	o	r	t	a	n	t	o
w	t	y	h	v	s	z	e	r	b
t	h	i	r	d	t	h	r	e	e
c	j	o	r	c	h	a	n	g	e
e	w	i	t	h	o	x	t	j	k
x	s	h	o	r	e	z	c	d	g
t	y	d	s	c	h	i	l	d	m
c	h	e	r	r	i	e	s	u	o
w	m	y	t	h	i	r	s	t	y
f	o	r	b	i	d	d	e	n	l

9e Wordmuddle

Write the words below next to the correct heading. Some of the words do not appear in the story.

        thumb   shore   clench

        bored   child   seventh

ch _____   _____

th _____   _____

or _____   _____

9f On a separate sheet of paper, draw a picture of Adam throwing a rope to his child in the canal. Colour in the picture then write a sentence underneath describing what is happening.

10. Consonant Clusters and Vowel Blending Spelling Made Easy
'ch', 'th', 'or' Level 2 Textbook
Pages 26 - 31

10a Reading Exercise

Adam's wife gets home. Her name is Cherry. Cherry works at the zoo. She has been chasing chimpanzees. Cherry is tired and a bit fed up. The chimpanzees' chatter makes a hell of a din! She is thankful to be home. Cherry throws down her jacket. She is very thirsty. She has been ordered by her boss to give a report on the chimpanzees. She thinks this will be boring. She finds chasing chimps more thrilling! Adam gives Cherry a big kiss on the cheek and tells her to sit down. Cherry says hello to Gus. Adam tells his wife that Gus is a friend that he met twenty years ago and that he is staying for supper. Cherry is happy. She loves visitors!

10b Reading Comprehension

Use the story to answer the questions:

1. What is Adam's wife's name?

2. What has Cherry been chasing at the zoo?

3. What has Cherry been ordered to do?

4. What does she think about writing the report?

5. What does Cherry feel about chasing chimps?

6. What does Cherry do with her jacket?

10c Picture – there are 3 words from the story in the picture below. Write the correct words underneath the box.

_____   _____   _____

10d Crossword

Use the clues and the story to fill in the boxes.

Across
1. Adam's wife. (6)
2. Exciting! (9)
3. This tells someone what happened. (6)

Down
1. A kind of ape. (10)
2. Running after someone. (7)
3. Not very exciting. (6)
4. To toss a ball. (5)

10e Wordsorting

Below are 6 new words. Write them next to the correct heading.

      sailor   platform   chestnut

      fourth   clench   length

ch _____ _____

th _____ _____

or _____ _____

10f On a separate sheet of paper draw a picture of Cherry chasing chimpanzees at the zoo. Colour it in then write a sentence underneath to describe what is happening.

11. Magic 'e' 1
'a-e', 'i-e'

Spelling Made Easy
Level 2 Textbook
Pages 32 – 35

11a Reading Exercise

Gus asks Cherry if the chimps are kept safe in a cage. Cherry tells him they have a very big cage and they can run about inside. They behave well and have plenty of space. They seem to quite like life in the zoo! Gus admires Cherry. She really likes her job, except when she must write a report. The three friends eat their supper. Cherry gets out a carton of chocolate ice cream. All of a sudden, they hear an alarm and sirens. Someone shouts 'Fire!' from the street. They drop their chocolate ice cream and race outside. The police and the fire brigade have arrived. A house is on fire. The flames are very big.

11b Reading Comprehension

Use the story to answer the questions:

1. Where are the chimps kept safe?

2. What do the chimps have plenty of?

3. How does Cherry think the chimps feel about life at the zoo?

4. What do the friends eat for pudding?

5. Who arrives to sort out the fire?

11c Pictures – use the story and the pictures to fill in the gaps.

The chimps _____ well and have lots of _____.

Cherry really _____ her job.

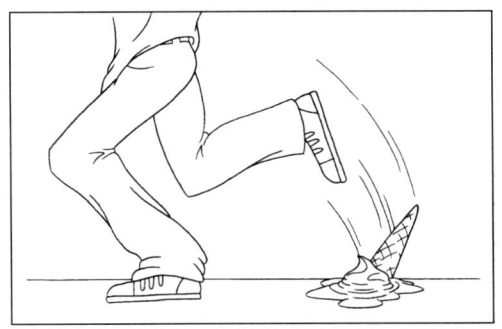

They drop their _____ cream and _____ outside.

The _____ are very big.

11d Wordsearch

There are 8 words from the story hidden in the box below. They go from left to right and top to bottom.

e	b	t	y	d	s	b	h	s	j
g	e	i	n	s	i	d	e	p	k
d	h	q	t	x	i	t	e	a	b
q	a	z	f	q	w	s	g	c	j
u	v	a	r	f	l	a	m	e	s
i	e	c	v	d	s	u	r	s	v
t	q	o	u	t	s	i	d	e	m
e	w	k	b	r	i	g	a	d	e
r	t	s	w	a	e	y	c	v	u
w	r	i	t	e	g	h	j	k	p

11e Wordmuddle

Write the words below next to the correct heading. Some of the words do not appear in the story.

cage   notice   beside

palace   admire   private

a-e _____   _____

i-e _____   _____

11f On a separate sheet of paper, draw a picture of either the fire brigade OR the police. Colour it in then write a sentence about it.

12. Magic 'e' 1
'a-e', 'i-e'

Spelling Made Easy
Level 2 Textbook
Pages 32 - 35

12a Reading Exercise

The fire looks bad. The family who live inside the house are all standing on the pavement. They are the Minhas family. A police officer is comforting the Minhas family. It seems that an electric wire caught fire by mistake. It then brushed the pages of a book on a table, which went up in flames. The Minhas family are not strangers to Adam and Cherry. They are quite good friends. Their children all like each other. Mr and Mrs Minhas have a boy and a girl. They often invite the family to their home for dinner. Adam, Cherry and Gus go over to the family and offer some advice and help. Mr Minhas tells them he cannot put a price on the damage from the fire. His wife is beside herself. She is glad her children are safe, but all their things are gone. Only the basement is left!

12b Reading Comprehension

Use the story to answer the questions:

1. What looks bad?

2. Where are the Minhas family standing?

3. What caught fire by mistake?

4. Where was the book?

5. What can Mr Minhas not put a price on?

6. What is left of their house?

12c Pictures — draw pictures of the words that appear underneath each box.

table	wire	pages

12d Crossword

Use the clues and the story to fill in the boxes.

Across
1. Light this to keep warm. (4)
2. Not in any danger. (4)
3. At the bottom of a house. (8)
4. Giving your opinions. (6)

Down
1. To ask someone to a party. (6)
2. Another word for smashing something up. (6)
3. A person you don't know. (8)
4. They keep order. (6)

12e Wordsorting

Below are 6 new words. Write them next to the correct heading.

tide   wages   disgrace

strange   practice   nineteen

a-e _____ _____ _____

i-e _____ _____ _____

12f Draw a picture of the Minhas family standing outside with Adam, Cherry and Gus. Think of names for the two Minhas children. Colour in the picture then label each person.

13. Magic 'e' 2
'o-e', 'u-e'

Spelling Made Easy
Level 2 Textbook
Pages 36 - 39

13a Reading Exercise

It is hopeless. The Minhas family are homeless. The street is full of smoke. Their clothes smell of smoke and the children choke up black dust. The fumes are bad too. Gus keeps choking himself! The family are not sure about the future. They will have to stay in a hotel. The children start to argue. Their Mum and Dad are very upset. Adam and Cherry take them to their own home to use the phone. Gus is left with the two arguing children. He sees a way to amuse them. He takes out a pen and a piece of paper and starts to draw. He captures them both in a picture. The children forget the fire and smile. The cartoon is really good!

13b Reading Comprehension

Use the story to answer the questions:

1. What is the street full of?

2. What smells of smoke?

3. How do the family feel about the future?

4. What do the children start to do?

5. What do the family use at Adam and Cherry's home?

6. What does Gus capture the Minhas children in?

13c Pictures

Write the correct word underneath each picture.

_____   _____   _____

13d Wordsearch

There are 8 words from the story hidden in the box below. They go from left to right and top to bottom.

a	m	u	s	e	g	s	e	l	h
x	c	a	p	t	u	r	e	m	o
d	t	h	s	r	z	w	c	k	p
t	f	u	t	u	r	e	h	j	e
z	u	v	f	s	e	k	o	z	l
q	m	w	f	e	s	u	k	n	e
o	e	v	s	p	g	d	e	x	s
f	s	d	p	h	o	n	e	p	s
t	y	x	d	a	v	d	e	m	w
h	o	m	e	l	e	s	s	g	d

13e Wordmuddle

Write the words below next to the correct heading. Some of the words do not appear in the story.

    hopeless   sure   explode

    excuse   alone   clue

o-e _____   _____

u-e _____   _____

13f On a separate sheet of paper draw a picture of the Minhas children smiling and Gus drawing the cartoon of them. Colour it in then write a sentence underneath to describe what is happening.

14. Magic 'e' 2
  'o-e', 'u-e'

Spelling Made Easy
Level 2 Textbook
Pages 36 - 39

14a Reading Exercise

Mr Minhas uses the phone in Adam's house to call his parents. He was hoping they could stay with them, but they are away. They will stay in a hotel for three days. Cherry makes some food for the family. She chops up potatoes and tomatoes and cooks a piece of fish. Cherry tells Mrs Minhas to be thankful that no one was injured in the blaze.
Gus arrives with the children. They are very excited about the picture. Everyone looks at Gus's cartoon. Adam had no clue that Gus was so good. It is very true to life! They all sit down for something to eat. Gus sees how close they all are. He hopes things will work out for them in the future.

14b Reading Comprehension

Use the story to answer the questions:

1. What does Mr Minhas use in Adam's house?

2. What two things does Cherry chop to cook with the fish?

3. What should Mrs Minhas be thankful for?

4. What does Gus see about the two families as they sit down?

5. What does Gus feel about the future of the Minhas family?

14c Picture – there are 3 words from the story in the picture below. Write the correct words underneath the box.

_____   _____   _____

14d Crossword

Use the clues and the story to fill in the boxes.

Across
1. Somewhere to stay on holiday. (5)
2. Round, red and goes on salad. (8)
3. Will help solve a riddle. (4)

Down
1. It may be a mobile or a landline. (5)
2. Not false. (4)
3. Hangs in a frame. (7)
4. Not far away. (5)

14e Wordsorting

Below are 6 new words. Write them next to the correct heading.

refuse   whole   continue

rode   choking   cure

o-e _____   _____   _____

u-e _____   _____   _____

14f On a separate sheet of paper, draw a picture of a plate of tomatoes and potatoes. Choose two other vegetables and draw them on the plate too. Colour in the picture then label each item.

15. Vowel Blending
'ai', 'oa', 'ir'

Spelling Made Easy
Level 2 Textbook
Pages 40 - 45

15a Reading Exercise

The cartoon has made the family forget to complain. Gus has a lump in his throat. Everyone seems happy. Suddenly, the thirteen-year-old girl complains of a pain in her leg. She moans and groans. Luckily Cherry has some first-aid training so the family are not afraid. The girl explains that as she was running from the house she fell and hurt herself. Cherry holds the girl firmly by the waist and has a good look at the hurt leg. The girl squirms a little but Cherry is well trained and she can see that it is not serious. She goes to the cupboard to get a plaster for the cut and the girl stops moaning.

15b Reading Comprehension

Use the story to answer the questions:

1. What has the cartoon made the family forget?

2. Where does Gus have a lump?

3. How old is the girl in the Minhas family?

4. What does she feel in her leg?

5. How does Cherry hold the girl's waist?

6. Where does Cherry go to get a plaster?

15c Pictures — use the story and the pictures to fill in the gaps.

The _____ moans and _____.

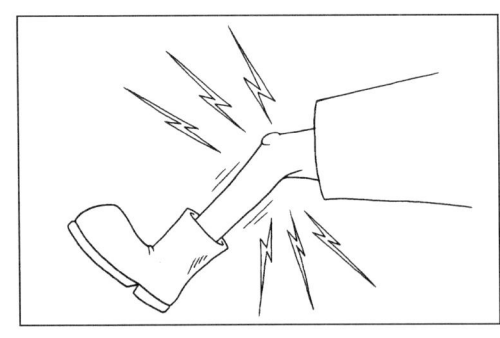

She has a _____ in her leg.

Cherry holds the girl _____ by the waist.

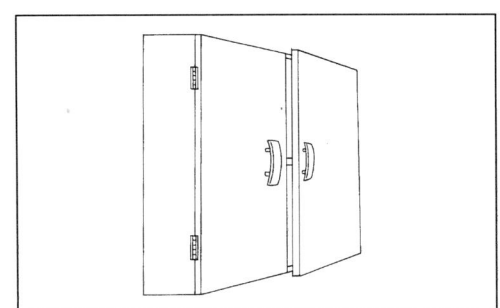
Cherry goes to the _____ to get a plaster.

15d Wordsearch

There are 9 words from the story hidden in the box below. They go from left to right and top to bottom.

e	t	r	a	i	n	i	n	g	z
t	h	i	r	t	e	e	n	j	k
f	w	e	v	s	g	w	v	s	u
g	b	x	g	r	w	h	m	o	n
i	c	p	a	i	n	m	o	u	a
r	y	l	w	q	c	b	a	u	f
l	z	a	f	t	s	e	n	h	r
m	f	i	r	s	t	a	i	d	a
w	e	n	f	g	s	v	y	l	i
f	g	s	q	u	i	r	m	s	d

15e Wordmuddle

Write the words below next to the correct heading. Some of the words do not appear in the story.

       complain   snail   throat

       circus   girl   roar

ai _____ _____ _____

oa _____ _____ _____

ir _____ _____ _____

15f On a separate sheet of paper draw a picture of Cherry holding the girl firmly by the waist. Colour it in then write a sentence underneath to describe what is happening.

16. Vowel Blending
'ai', 'oa', 'ir'

Spelling Made Easy
Level 2 Textbook
Pages 40 - 45

16a Reading Exercise

Gus thinks he should go. He goes to the cloakroom to find his coat. He sees lots of coats – an overcoat, a raincoat and a dufflecoat. He cannot see his coat. Gus fails to see his own coat anywhere on the rail. He turns to see Adam waiting for him. Adam wants to know why Gus is leaving. Gus tries to explain that he would like to remain with his new friends, but he does not want to be in the way. Adam is quite firm that Gus must stay. They all love his cartoon and want him to do more. Gus grabs a pen and twirls it with his fingers. He starts to draw and forgets all about his coat!

16b Reading Comprehension

Use the story to answer the questions:

1. Where does Gus go to find his coat?

2. Name three different coats from the story.

3. Where does Gus fail to see his coat?

4. What does Gus turn to see Adam doing?

5. Adam is quite _____ that Gus must stay.

6. What does Gus do with the pen when he grabs it?

16c Pictures – draw a picture of each sentence in the box.

Gus twirls the pen.

Gus sees lots of coats on a rail.

16d Crossword

Use the clues and the story to fill in the boxes.

Across
1. A place to keep hats and coats. (9)
2. A twist or spin. (5)
3. Something to hold on to or hang things on. (4)
4. A strong word can make you sound this way. (4)

Down
1. Wear this to keep out the cold. (4)
2. To stay. (6)
3. To make someone understand. (7)

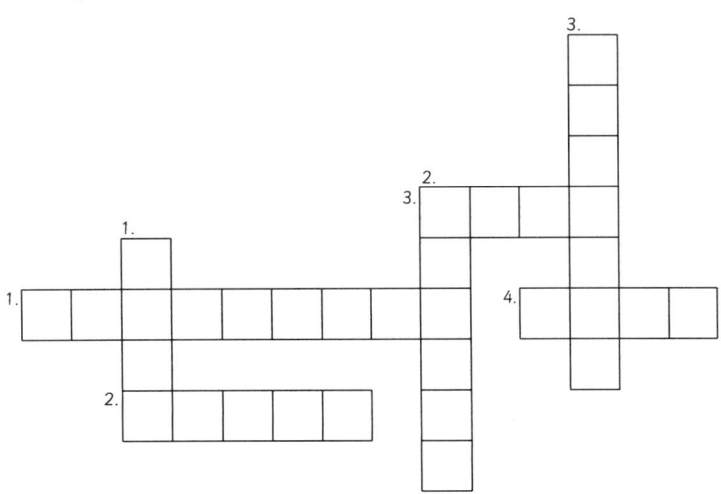

16e Wordsorting

Below are 6 new words. Write them next to the correct heading.

first   oar   trail

float   main   circuit

ai _____   _____

oa _____   _____

ir _____   _____

16f On a separate sheet of paper, draw a picture of yourself wearing your favourite outfit. It may be a skirt, a shirt or a coat. Colour it in then label each item of clothing.

17. Vowel Blending
'ou', 'ea', 'ur'

Spelling Made Easy
Level 2 Textbook
Pages 46 - 51

17a Reading Exercise

Adam, Cherry and the Minhas family do not make a sound as Gus draws. They look at Gus in his dirty old jeans and shirt. He looks more like a burglar than an artist! They are surprised by how talented he is. The cartoons seem to come to him so easily – a nose here, an ear there and a cartoon appears of Adam and Cherry standing next to a fountain. Gus then draws the Minhas family. They love it so much they offer to pay Gus a thousand pounds. This is a huge amount! Gus does not even have a bank account. A policeman disturbs them. He wants to talk to the Minhas family. He tells them that their house is OK, but that their curtains and furniture are badly burnt.

17b Reading Comprehension

Use the story to answer the questions:

1. What does Gus look more like than an artist?

2. What do the Minhas family feel about Gus's talent?

3. What are Adam and Cherry standing next to in Gus's cartoon?

4. How much money do the Minhas family offer to pay Gus for his drawing?

5. Are the cartoons easy or hard for Gus to draw?

17c Pictures

Write the correct word underneath each picture.

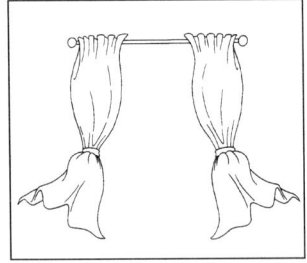 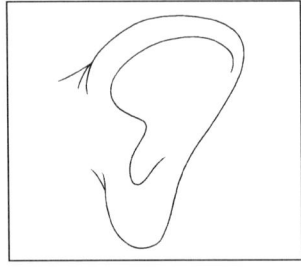 

17d Wordsearch

There are 9 words from the story hidden in the box below. They go from left to right and top to bottom.

a	d	s	s	o	u	n	d	p	e
m	w	a	c	c	o	u	n	t	a
o	q	v	c	s	g	h	x	m	s
u	z	x	s	a	r	j	e	k	i
n	f	b	u	r	n	t	a	m	l
t	q	r	o	s	g	y	r	p	y
e	t	f	h	l	v	x	c	n	m
f	u	r	n	i	t	u	r	e	u
g	y	d	c	s	j	e	a	n	s
p	w	d	i	s	t	u	r	b	s

17e Wordmuddle

Write the words below next to the correct heading. Some of the words do not appear in the story.

    sound   disturb   hour

    seasons   jeans   pursue

ou _____ _____

ea _____ _____

ur _____ _____

17f On a separate sheet of paper draw a picture of Gus in his dirty jeans and old shirt. Colour in the picture then write a sentence underneath about what you think of Gus the tramp.

18. Vowel Blending
  'ou', 'ea', 'ur'

**Spelling Made Easy
Level 2 Textbook
Pages 46 - 51**

18a Reading Exercise

Cherry murmurs to Adam urgently. She says they have three spare rooms. She thinks Gus and the Minhas family should stay with them. They all feel weary and sleepy. The Minhas family don't really want to go to a hotel, and Gus has no home. They are so pleased to stay as the hour is late and it is chilly outside. Cherry puts on the central heating. Gus feels surrounded by friends and is so happy. He has a thousand pounds and a room for the night! He thinks the Minhas family are very brave. They have had a terrible night and they are not sour or mean. Adam shows Gus his room. It has velvet curtains with pictures of leaves. The bed is nice and big. Gus is glad because he can curl up and sleep.

18b Reading Comprehension

Use the story to answer the questions:

1. What does Cherry do urgently?

2. They all feel _____ and sleepy.

3. How does the Minhas family feel about staying?

4. Where is it chilly?

5. Why is Gus glad that the bed is big?

6. How much money does Gus have?

18c Picture – there are 3 words from the story in the picture below. Write the correct words underneath the box.

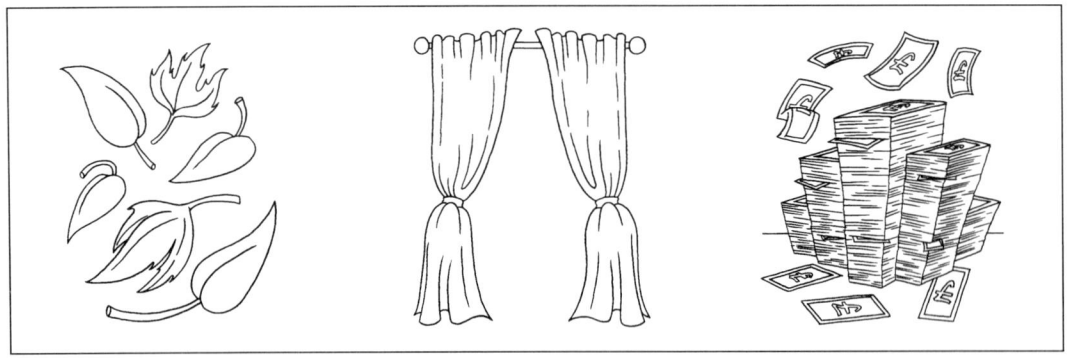

_____   _____   _____

18d Crossword

Use the clues and the story to fill in the boxes.

Across
1. Keeps the house warm. (7)
2. Use these to cover the windows. (8)
3. To talk in a low voice. (6)
4. They fall from the trees in autumn. (6)

Down
1. 60 minutes. (4)
2. It must be done now! (6)
3. Another word for nasty or unkind. (4)
4. Not sweet. (4)

18e Wordsorting

Below are 6 new words. Write them next to the correct heading.

lounge   surname   gear

leaning   flour   turban

ou _____   _____

ea _____   _____

ur _____   _____

18f On a separate sheet of paper draw a picture of Gus's new bedroom with its velvet curtains and nice, big bed. Colour in the picture then label each item in the room.

19. Vowel Blending
   'aw', 'oi', 'er'

Spelling Made Easy
Level 2 Textbook
Pages 52 - 57

19a Reading Exercise

The next morning everyone meets in the kitchen for bacon, eggs and toast with strawberry jam. They have all had a good sleep. The Minhas family are nervous about seeing the house in the day. They are certain it will be very bad but it is unavoidable. Gus feels awful for them. There has been a frost but it has thawed. Mr And Mrs Minhas need to speak to their lawyer. Cherry must go to get groceries from the supermarket. Adam has to go to the choir he joined the week before. Gus says he will stay with the Minhas children. He wraps the leftover food in kitchen foil and then sits down to do some more drawing. The children sit down with him. They love Gus.

19b Reading Comprehension

Use the story to answer the questions:

1. What sort of jam do they have on their toast?

2. How do the Minhas family feel about seeing the house?

3. What does Gus feel for the family?

4. What does Cherry need to get from the supermarket?

5. Where does Adam have to go?

6. What does Gus use to wrap up the leftover food?

19c Pictures – use the story and the pictures to fill in the gaps.

There has been a frost, but it has _____.

Cherry gets groceries from the _____.

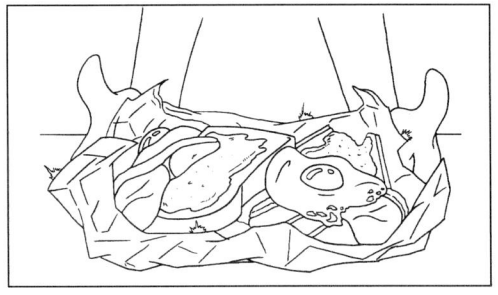

Gus wraps the _____ food in kitchen _____.

Gus sits down to do some more _____.

19d Wordsearch

There are 9 words from the story hidden in the box below. They go from left to right and top to bottom.

u	n	a	v	o	i	d	a	b	l	e
d	f	w	g	h	r	w	x	o	w	x
b	n	f	e	r	a	b	x	u	r	c
v	t	u	j	o	i	n	e	d	k	e
l	o	l	c	s	g	y	c	g	s	r
a	t	y	z	w	j	k	h	o	l	t
w	g	h	d	x	e	t	o	k	x	a
y	g	r	o	c	e	r	i	e	s	i
e	h	t	j	k	h	o	r	p	s	n
r	a	d	r	a	w	i	n	g	n	d
a	n	e	r	v	o	u	s	u	i	s

19e Wordmuddle

Write the words below next to the correct heading. Some of the words do not appear in the story.

        certain   exercise   thawed

        jaw   choir   poison

aw _____ _____

oi _____ _____

er _____ _____

19f On a separate sheet of paper draw a picture of a big plate of eggs, bacon and toast with strawberry jam. Think of two more things you eat for breakfast and draw them too. Colour in the picture then label each item.

20. Vowel Blending
 'aw', 'oi', 'er'

**Spelling Made Easy
Level 2 Textbook
Pages 52 - 57**

20a Reading Exercise

Gus is so happy to be drawing again. He sees how withdrawn he was before meeting Adam. Life seemed a bit pointless, but now he can help people. His drawings and cartoons have made his friends happy. It took their minds off awful things. Gus feels that helping others will give him an interesting life. He can remember before his crash how different he was. He now understands how to use his gift for drawing. The thirteen-year-old girl needs some ointment for her leg. Her mother and father are still talking on the phone to their lawyer. Gus goes to the cupboard. He avoids the rat poison and gets the ointment. He makes a hanky moist and dabs the girl's cut leg. It stings and she starts bawling!

20b Reading Comprehension

Use the story to answer the questions:

1. What is Gus happy about?

2. How did life seem to Gus before he started drawing again?

3. What kind of life does Gus think he will have through helping people?

4. What does the girl need for her leg?

5. Gus now _____ how to use his gift.

6. What does the girl start doing when the ointment stings?

20c Pictures – draw a picture of each sentence in the box.

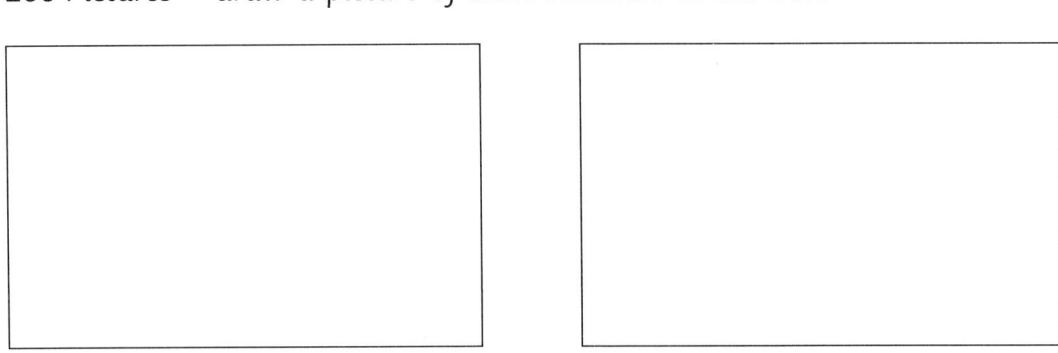

Mr and Mrs Minhas are still talking on the phone to their lawyer.

Gus avoids the poison and gets the ointment.

20d Crossword

Use the clues and the story to fill in the boxes.

Across
1. Another word for terrible or bad. (5)
2. To think of something in the past. (8)
3. To make a little damp. (5)
4. A dangerous substance. (6)

Down
1. Not the same. (9)
2. You make this with paper and pencil. (7)
3. Crying loudly. (7)

20e Wordsorting

Below are 6 new words. Write them next to the correct heading.

prawn   oil   Germany

spider   sprawl   voice

aw _____   _____

oi _____   _____

er _____   _____

20f On a separate sheet of paper draw a picture of something you did at the weekend that you really enjoyed. Colour in the picture then write a sentence underneath to describe what is happening.

21. Vowel Blending
   'al', 'ea' (short e), 'ow'

Spelling Made Easy
Level 2 Textbook
Pages 58 - 63

21a Reading Exercise

The girl gradually stops her crying. Her leg is not too bad so she will not have to go to the hospital, although she is still in pain. Apart from her leg she is quite healthy. She is feeling a little drowsy. Gus is a big, powerful man. He picks her up. To Gus she feels like a feather. He puts her to bed for a few hours. Gus feels he would like a shower. He is a bit sweaty. He grabs a towel and heads off to the bathroom. There is an almighty crash. The little Minhas boy has been a bit rowdy all morning and now he has broken a mirror. Gus threatens to tell his Mum and Dad if he does not sit down and be good. Gus cleans up the mirror quietly and stealthily. He winks at the boy and says it will be their secret.

21b Reading Comprehension

Use the story to answer the questions:

1. In what way does the girl stop her crying?

2. How is she feeling? (Clue!! Another word for sleepy)

3. How does she feel to Gus when he picks her up?

4. What does Gus grab on his way to the bathroom?

5. How has the Minhas boy been all morning?

6. Gus cleans up the mirror quietly and _____.

21c Pictures

Write the correct word underneath each picture.

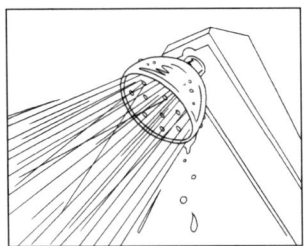  

_____   _____   _____

21d Wordsearch

There are 9 words from the story hidden in the box below. They go from left to right and top to bottom.

d	f	h	o	s	p	i	t	a	l	j	h
r	o	v	w	h	q	a	c	b	t	s	e
m	c	r	h	o	h	d	o	w	n	w	a
t	f	g	s	w	j	k	l	t	y	c	l
h	w	q	c	e	z	g	r	h	j	s	t
r	e	u	i	r	v	x	e	b	m	w	h
e	p	o	w	e	r	f	u	l	x	e	y
a	a	d	s	f	b	t	s	e	g	a	m
t	b	g	h	d	e	s	w	t	p	t	u
e	d	a	l	m	i	g	h	t	y	y	w
n	q	c	f	a	g	r	x	h	j	f	s
s	t	g	r	a	d	u	a	l	l	y	u

21e Wordmuddle

Write the words below next to the correct heading. Some of the words do not appear in the story.

    almighty   treasure   towel

    musical   allow   threatens

al _____   _____

ea _____   _____

ow _____   _____

21f On a separate sheet of paper draw a picture of the little boy breaking the mirror into a thousand pieces and Gus stealthily cleaning it up. Colour in the picture then write a sentence underneath to explain what is happening.

22. Vowel Blending
  'al', 'ea' (short e), 'ow'

Spelling Made Easy
Level 2 Textbook
Pages 58 - 63

22a Reading Exercise

Cherry arrives home from the supermarket. She unpacks the shopping. She has got some washing-powder so that the Minhas family can clean their dirty clothes. She has also got some nice food for lunch. She tells Mr and Mrs Minhas that the weather outside is fine and bright. The sun is out. Although Mr and Mrs Minhas are sad about the house, they are healthy and wealthy. They always sort things out. Cherry makes some soup for lunch. She gets out an electric mixer and plugs it into a power point. Soon it will be ready. Adam is home from his choir practice and Gus is out of the shower. They all sit down to eat. After lunch, Gus gets his flute and starts to play a happy tune. It brings everyone great pleasure. They did not know he was musical! It seems to come naturally. The children are allowed some sweets.

22b Reading Comprehension

Use the story to answer the questions:

1. What can the Minhas family clean their clothes with?

2. Mr and Mrs Minhas are sad, but they also _____ and _____.

3. What does Cherry plug her electric mixer into?

4. What is fine and bright?

5. What didn't the people know about Gus?

22c Picture – Write the correct words underneath the box.

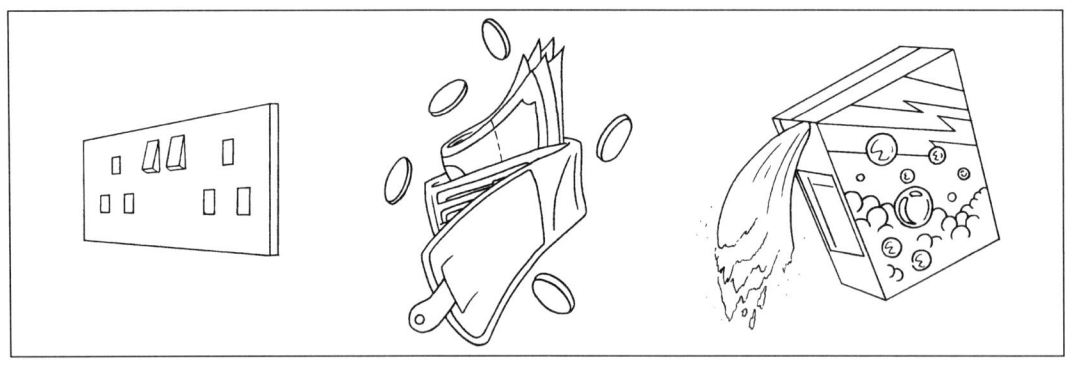

_____   _____   _____

22d Crossword

Use the clues and the story to fill in the boxes.

Across
1. A fine dust. (6)
2. An ability to hold a tune. (7)
3. When something is easy, it comes _____. (9)
4. Sun, rain, snow, wind. (7)

Down
1. You have permission. (7)
2. Not sick or ill. (7)
3. Lots of money. (7)

22e Wordsorting

Below are 6 new words. Write them next to the correct heading.

criminal   leather   tower

vowel   annually   ahead

al _____   _____

ea _____   _____

ow _____   _____

22f On a separate sheet of paper draw a picture of Gus playing a tune on his flute and everyone taking great pleasure in his musical abilities. Colour in the picture then write a sentence underneath to describe what is happening.

23. Silent letters, a (ar) and Endings

**Spelling Made Easy
Level 2 Textbook
Pages 64 - 69**

23a Reading Exercise

Adam, Cherry and the Minhas family all listen to Gus playing the flute. It is almost as if they are in a trance. They did not know he could play so beautifully. It is wonderful. Gus finishes the tune and tells them he wrote it himself. He is a really talented guy! The music has made the Minhas family feel that it may be possible to handle the situation with their burnt house. They are all very calm. Music can certainly be very powerful! Suddenly the phone rings. It is Mr Minhas's Aunty and Uncle. They want to be helpful. They have a very big house. They want the Minhas family to live with them until they can find a new house. The Minhas family's prayers have been answered! They are very thankful. Cherry fetches some raspberries and sweet biscuits to celebrate.

23b Reading Comprehension

Use the story to answer the questions:

1. What did the people not know about Gus's flute playing abilities?

2. What does Gus tell them about the tune?

3. What does the story say music can be?

4. Who calls the Minhas family on the phone?

5. What two things does Cherry fetch for them to celebrate?

23c Pictures – use the story and the pictures to fill in the gaps.

It is almost as if they are in a _____.

Gus is a really talented _____!

_____ the phone rings.

Cherry fetches some _____ and sweet _____.

23d Wordsearch

There are 10 words from the story hidden in the box below. They go from left to right and top to bottom.

f	l	i	s	t	e	n	x	n	p
a	n	s	w	e	r	e	d	l	o
q	w	c	g	s	h	g	j	k	s
f	o	c	b	k	n	o	w	o	s
a	z	a	d	f	t	s	b	g	i
m	h	l	w	r	o	t	e	u	b
i	u	m	c	k	s	l	m	y	l
l	i	u	a	u	n	t	y	n	e
y	t	y	x	s	b	g	s	u	o
b	t	h	a	n	k	f	u	l	w

23e Wordmuddle

Write the words below next to the correct heading. Some of the words do not appear in the story.

       calm   soften   biscuit

       sensibly   powerful   passport

Silent letter _____   _____

a _____   _____

Ending _____   _____

23f Think about the words of your favourite song. On a separate sheet of paper, draw a picture to illustrate one part of the song. Colour in the picture then write a sentence underneath to explain the picture.

24. Silent letters, a (ar) and Endings

**Spelling Made Easy
Level 2 Textbook
Pages 64 - 69**

24a Reading Exercise

The Minhas family feel it is time to leave Adam, Cherry and Gus. They have been guests for long enough. With the help of their friends, and Aunty and Uncle Minhas, they will be able to handle the terrible problem. Mr Minhas says they will buy a plot of land and build their own dream home. They tell Adam, Cherry and Gus to come and visit them often. They would like to listen to Gus's music and look at his cartoons again. Gus feels a knot in his tummy. He has had a wonderful time, even though the fire was terrible. The Minhas family put on their coats and fasten up the buttons. They get into a taxi. They all have one last glance back at their old house and off they go! They wave back to their friends.

24b Reading Comprehension

Use the story to answer the questions:

1. What do the Minhas family feel they have been for long enough?

2. How much do the Minhas family tell the others to visit?

3. What does Gus feel in his tummy?

4. What sort of time has Gus had with his new friends?

5. What do the Minhas family do with the buttons on their coats?

24c Pictures – draw a picture of each sentence in the box.

The Minhas family fasten the buttons on their coats.

Gus feels a knot in his tummy.

24d Crossword

Use the clues and the story to fill in the boxes.

Across
1. To cope with a situation. (6)
2. A quick look. (6)
3. To hear. (6)

Down
1. Someone staying in your house. (6)
2. This connects two bits of string. (4)
3. To do up buttons. (6)
4. A group of people who are related. (6)

24e Wordsorting

Below are 6 new words. Write them next to the correct heading.

simple   calf   tongue
honest   horribly France

Silent letter _____   _____

a   _____   _____

Ending   _____   _____

24f On a separate sheet of paper draw a picture of your dream home. Colour in the picture then write a short paragraph describing the drawing and explaining why it is your dream home.

25. Various

**Spelling Made Easy
Level 2 Textbook
Pages 70 - 75**

25a Reading Exercise

Adam, Cherry and Gus go back inside the house. Gus starts to put his coat on but Adam asks him to wait. Adam and Cherry go into the kitchen to have a discussion. Gus feels a bit nervous, but it is only polite to obey Adam's request. It all seems very serious. Gus is confused because he doesn't know what is going on. He thinks he may be in trouble, but the fire was not his fault. He has not been naughty. Adam and Cherry come out of the kitchen. They look very serious and are silent. Then they start to laugh. They want to invite Gus to live with them in their house. Gus feels so happy! He now feels ridiculous for feeling so nervous. A few days ago he had no friends and nowhere to live. Now he has lots of friends and a home!

25b Reading Comprehension

Use the story to answer the questions:

1. Why do Adam and Cherry go into the kitchen?

2. How does Gus feel about it?

3. What is it polite for Gus to do?

4. What do Adam and Cherry start to do after they come out of the kitchen?

5. How does Gus feel about his part in the fire?

6. How does Gus feel about being nervous once he understands what is happening?

25c Pictures (Clue—all these words are feelings or actions based on feelings)
Write the correct word underneath each picture.

_____   _____   _____

25d Wordsearch

There are 8 words from the story hidden in the box below. They go from left to right and top to bottom.

a	c	n	o	w	h	e	r	e	x
w	n	a	u	g	h	t	y	y	n
o	d	s	a	c	v	b	a	u	t
g	h	o	d	j	k	u	g	f	c
r	i	d	i	c	u	l	o	u	s
w	t	f	e	v	b	s	g	t	j
u	o	a	v	p	o	l	i	t	e
x	b	u	z	c	g	d	y	u	o
p	e	l	o	s	i	l	e	n	t
m	y	t	s	e	r	i	o	u	s

25e Wordmuddle

Write the words below next to the correct heading. Some of the words do not appear in the story.

author   obey   discussion

iron   jealous   envious

au _____   -ous _____

-ious _____   -sion _____

i _____   o _____

25f Divide a separate sheet of paper into four equal parts. In each part, draw a picture of your face looking serious, nervous, curious and laughing. Colour in the pictures then label each one with the correct word.

26. Various

**Spelling Made Easy
Level 2 Textbook
Pages 70 - 75**

26a Reading Exercise

Adam, Cherry and Gus hug each other. One of Adam and Cherry's daughters arrives home on her bicycle. Her name is Clara. She is at Primary School down the road, but she has been staying with her Grandma. Her Grandma had been on an excursion to Australia and had brought Clara some delicious sweets as a present. She hugs her Mum and Dad, and then she notices Gus. Clara is curious about who he is. Adam and Cherry explain everything. Clara thinks it is marvellous to have a new member of the family. Cherry makes sausages with cauliflower and cheese sauce for tea. This is Gus's favourite meal. He thinks about his thousand pounds. He thinks he might buy a motor-bike and go on little excursions. After supper he draws a huge cartoon of his new family. Adam says they will keep it safe as it is very precious. Gus thinks this is the best day of his whole life!

26b Reading Comprehension

Use the story to answer the questions:

1. What does Clara arrive home on?

2. Where has her Grandma been?

3. How does the story describe the sweets Clara has?

4. What does Cherry make for tea?

5. What might Gus buy with his thousand pounds?

6. Why does Adam want to keep Gus's cartoon safe?

26c Picture – Write the correct words underneath the box.

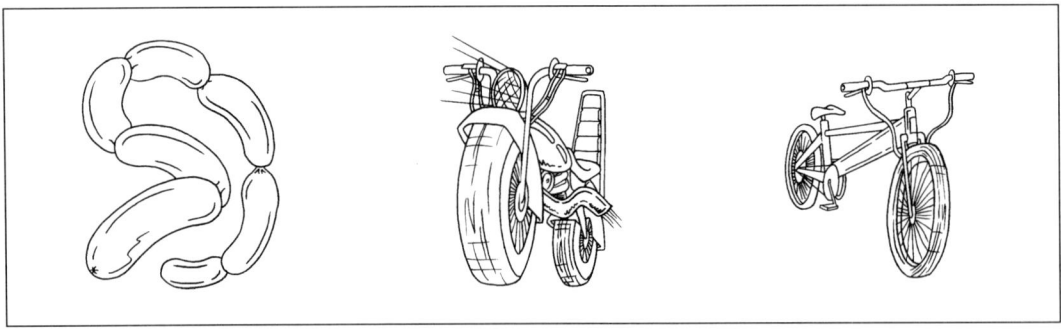

_____   _____   _____

26d Crossword

Use the clues and the story to fill in the boxes.

Across
1. To suddenly see something. (6)
2. Trips or outings. (10)
3. A vehicle with two wheels and pedals. (7)
4. Something that is important to you. (8)

Down
1. A liquid to pour on food. (5)
2. A vegetable that goes with cheese sauce. (11)
3. To feel interested. (5)

26e Wordsorting

Below are 6 new words. Write them next to the correct heading.

ghost   tremendous   admission

anxious   diamond   taught

au _____   -ous _____

-ious _____   -sion _____

i _____   o _____

26f On a separate sheet of paper, draw a picture of Gus, Adam, Cherry and Clara enjoying plates of sausages and cauliflower with cheese sauce. Colour in the picture then write a sentence underneath to describe what is happening.

ANSWERS (pages 2-3)

1. Short Vowel Sounds
   'a', 'o', 'i'

Spelling Made Easy
Level 2 Textbook
Pages 6 - 11

1b Reading Comprehension

Correct answers should include the following key words.

1. **Badger**
2. **A jogger**
3. **On a bridge**
4. **Drifts**
5. **In his tracks**
6. **Bossy**

1c Pictures

bridge   **canal**   **dog**

1d Wordsearch

t	r	a	m	p	h	j	e	r	v
s	x	q	f	y	n	o	t	h	l
r	d	i	s	t	r	u	s	t	b
f	o	t	e	c	v	m	a	n	z
s	p	o	t	s	g	x	z	q	k
w	y	u	c	o	n	t	e	n	t
d	m	i	s	f	i	t	j	a	e
u	f	a	e	f	a	m	i	l	y
c	r	o	s	s	t	x	y	o	v
q	o	g	d	i	s	m	i	s	s

1e Wordmuddle

a	**angry**	**tracks**
o	**bossy**	**knock**
i	**drifts**	**mistake**

ANSWERS (pages 4-5)

2. Short Vowel Sounds
'a', 'o', 'i'

Spelling Made Easy
Level 2 Textbook
Pages 6 - 11

2b Reading Comprehension

Correct answers should include the following key words.

1. **Adam**
2. **Contact**
3. **Disco or rugby match**
4. **Knocked out**
5. **Shop**
6. **Dismiss him**

2c Picture

    disco   **cap**   **jogger**

2d Crossword

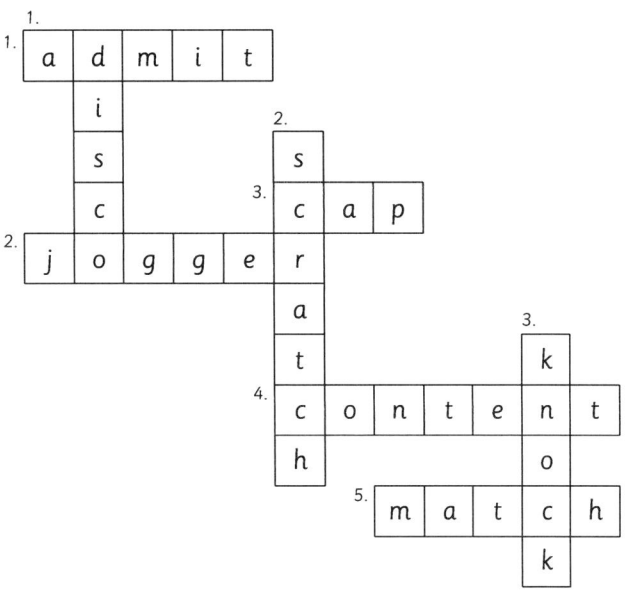

2e Wordsorting

    a   **attack**   **plastic**
    o   **prompt**   **glossy**
    i   **minimum**   **wrist**

ANSWERS (pages 6-7)

3. Short Vowel Sounds
   'e', 'u'

Spelling Made Easy
Level 2 Textbook
Pages 12 - 15

3b Reading Comprehension

Correct answers should include the following key words.

1. **They look at him with disgust**
2. **Distrust/judge him**
3. **Hectic**
4. **Seventeen**
5. **Exit**
6. **It is unjust**

3c Pictures

The teashop is **hectic**.

A **hundred** pounds is missing.

There is a **sudden** shout.

People want to **expel** Gus from the teashop.

3d Wordsearch

o	**p**	r	t	d	v	b	n	d	**e**
c	**u**	s	z	x	q	p	f	d	**l**
u	**b**	s	**u**	**d**	**d**	**e**	**n**	c	**e**
l	**l**	k	g	h	m	y	r	f	**c**
p	**i**	**d**	**i**	**s**	**t**	**r**	**u**	**s**	**t**
r	**c**	v	b	g	d	s	e	h	**r**
i	x	**s**	**u**	**s**	**p**	**e**	**c**	**t**	**i**
t	f	c	o	z	r	y	u	j	**c**
z	w	r	u	**e**	**x**	**p**	**e**	**l**	k
e	**x**	**p**	**e**	**c**	**t**	o	l	v	b

3e Wordmuddle

e	hedge	seven	electric
u	unpack	culprit	struck

ANSWERS (pages 8-9)

4. Short Vowel Sounds
'e', 'u'

**Spelling Made Easy
Level 2 Textbook
Pages 12 - 15**

4b Reading Comprehension

Correct answers should include the following key words.

1. **Unwell**
2. **Unplug it**
3. **Onto a ledge**
4. **He expects it**
5. **Stuck up for him**
6. **He had just met him**

4d Crossword

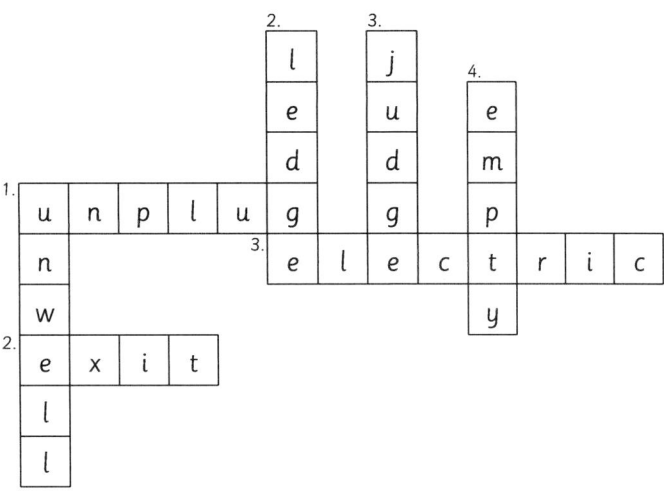

4e Wordsorting

e	**second**	**exist**	**smell**
u	**umbrella**	**until**	**skull**

57

ANSWERS (pages 10-11)

5. Consonant Clusters and Phonemes
'ck', 'ee', 'oo'

Spelling Made Easy
Level 2 Textbook
Pages 16 - 21

5b Reading Comprehension

Correct answers should include the following key words.

1. **Gloomy**
2. **Gives it a squeeze**
3. **Ducks**
4. **Sweets**
5. **In his pocket**
6. **It is crooked**

5c Pictures

    ducklings   **tooth**   **sweets**

5d Wordsearch

t	y	r	s	c	b	**f**	**o**	**o**	**d**
h	**n**	**o**	**o**	**n**	g	j	f	s	r
v	b	**s**	**w**	**e**	**e**	**t**	**s**	x	z
w	g	r	y	d	s	**b**	**a**	**c**	**k**
d	**u**	**c**	**k**	s	u	i	f	d	s
g	t	e	**f**	**o**	**o**	**l**	p	g	s
c	x	**f**	**e**	**e**	**l**	**s**	w	d	f
e	g	d	s	f	o	o	h	c	d
s	**e**	**e**	s	z	x	**m**	**o**	**o**	**d**
p	**o**	**c**	**k**	**e**	**t**	w	q	h	r

5e Wordmuddle

    ck   **trickle**   **duckling**
    ee   **squeeze**   **free**
    oo   **balloon**   **swoop**

ANSWERS (pages 12-13)

6. Consonant Clusters and Phonemes
'ck', 'ee', 'oo'

Spelling Made Easy
Level 2 Textbook
Pages 16 - 21

6b Reading Comprehension

Correct answers should include the following key words.

1. **Cook some lunch**
2. **Pickle**
3. **Greedy**
4. **Cheese**
5. **Jacket pocket**
6. **Gloomy**

6c Crossword

jacket   **cheese**   **tooth**

6d Crossword

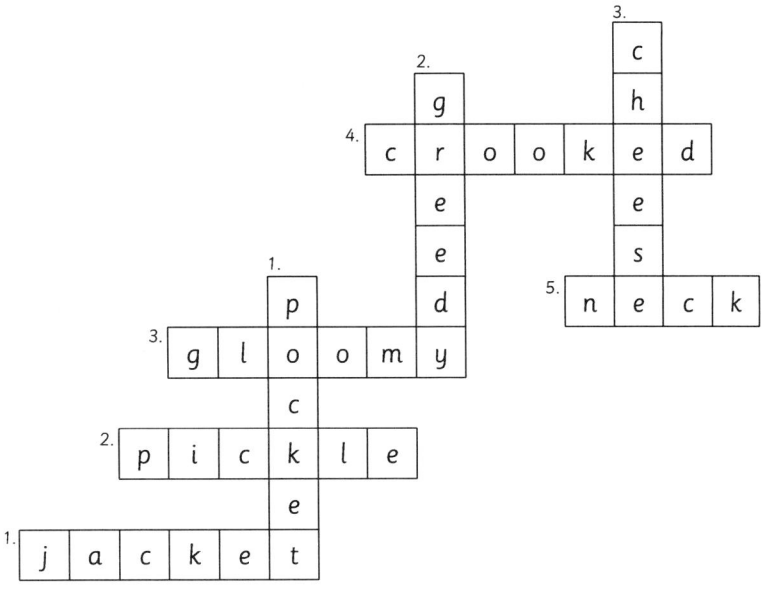

6e Wordsorting

ck	**ticket**	**smack**
ee	**knee**	**sleeve**
oo	**scoop**	**choose**

ANSWERS (pages 14-15)

7. Consonant Clusters and Phonemes
   'ar', 'sh'

Spelling Made Easy
Level 2 Textbook
Pages 22 - 25

7b Reading Comprehension

Correct answers should include the following key words.

1. **Shake/shudders**
2. **No harm**
3. **Selfish**
4. **Market**
5. **Crash**
6. **Arm**

7c Pictures

Gus starts to **shudder** and **shake** his head.

Gus would sell his cartoons at the **market**.

Gus had lots of friends and lots of **cash**.

Gus had a crash in his **car** and broke his **arm**.

7d Wordsearch

c	d	f	g	w	x	a	c	f	j
a	k	l	f	s	v	r	b	m	s
s	s	h	a	k	e	t	c	a	r
h	u	q	w	x	s	i	z	v	b
t	y	d	s	h	j	s	k	m	d
x	h	a	r	m	w	t	d	o	r
j	f	x	m	a	r	k	e	t	w
s	e	l	f	i	s	h	m	c	e
v	h	s	r	o	f	e	t	x	a
r	t	s	x	f	l	a	s	h	b

7e Wordmuddle

| ar | **harm** | **alarm** | **carpet** |
| sh | **selfish** | **mash** | **punish** |

ANSWERS (pages 16-17)

8. Consonant Clusters and Phonemes
 'ar', 'sh'

Spelling Made Easy
Level 2 Textbook
Pages 22 - 25

8b Reading Comprehension

Correct answers should include the following key words.

1. **Shocked, sad**
2. **Alarmed**
3. **Scar**
4. **Shrimps, mash, parsnips**
5. **Cartoon**

8d Crossword

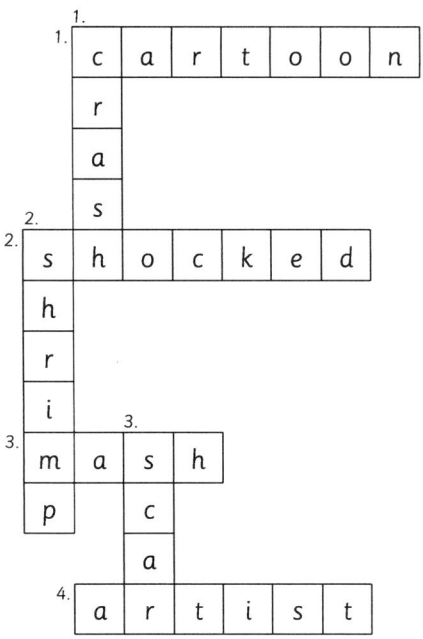

8e Wordsorting

ar	**dark**	**snarl**	**department**
sh	**finish**	**shaking**	**splash**

61

ANSWERS (pages 18-19)

9. Consonant Clusters and Vowel Blending
'ch', 'th', 'or'

Spelling Made Easy
Level 2 Textbook
Pages 26 - 31

9b Reading Comprehension

Correct answers should include the following key words.

1. **Throats**
2. **Cherries**
3. **Three**
4. **Doctor**
5. **Threw/Shore**
6. **Forbidden**

9c Pictures

cherries   thumb   doctor

9d Wordsearch

i	m	p	o	r	t	a	n	t	o
w	t	y	h	v	s	z	e	r	b
t	h	i	r	d	t	h	r	e	e
c	j	o	r	c	h	a	n	g	e
e	w	i	t	h	o	x	t	j	k
x	s	h	o	r	e	z	c	d	g
t	y	d	s	c	h	i	l	d	m
c	h	e	r	r	i	e	s	u	o
w	m	y	t	h	i	r	s	t	y
f	o	r	b	i	d	d	e	n	l

9e Wordmuddle

ch	**clench**	**child**
th	**thumb**	**seventh**
or	**shore**	**bored**

ANSWERS (pages 20-21)

10. Consonant Clusters and Vowel Blending Spelling Made Easy
'ch', 'th', 'or'   Level 2 Textbook
Pages 26 - 31

10b Reading Comprehension

Correct answers should include the following key words.

1. **Cherry**
2. **Chimpanzees**
3. **Report**
4. **Boring**
5. **Thrilling**
6. **Throws**

10c Picture

chimpanzee   **visitor**   **thirsty**

10d Crossword

						3.			4.	
		2.				b			t	
		c				o			h	
		h			3. r	e	p	o	r	t
1.		a				i			o	
	c	s				n			w	
2. t	h	r	i	l	l	i	n	g		
	i	n								
	m	g								
	p									
	a									
	n									
	z									
1. c	h	e	r	r	y					
	e									

10e Wordsorting

ch	**chestnut**	**clench**
th	**length**	**fourth**
or	**platform**	**sailor**

ANSWERS (pages 22-23)

11. Magic 'e' 1
'a-e', 'i-e'

Spelling Made Easy
Level 2 Textbook
Pages 32 - 35

11b Reading Comprehension

Correct answers should include the following key words.

1. **Cage**
2. **Space**
3. **Quite like**
4. **Chocolate ice cream**
5. **Fire brigade**

11c Pictures

The chimps **behave** well and have lots of **space**.

They drop their **ice** cream and **race** outside.

Cherry really **likes** her job.

The **flames** are very big.

11d Wordsearch

e	**b**	t	y	d	s	b	h	**s**	j
g	**e**	**i**	**n**	**s**	**i**	**d**	**e**	**p**	k
d	**h**	q	t	x	i	t	e	**a**	b
q	**a**	z	f	q	w	s	g	**c**	j
u	**v**	a	r	**f**	**l**	**a**	**m**	**e**	**s**
i	**e**	c	v	d	s	u	r	s	v
t	q	**o**	**u**	**t**	**s**	**i**	**d**	**e**	m
e	w	k	**b**	**r**	**i**	**g**	**a**	**d**	**e**
r	t	s	w	a	e	y	c	v	u
w	**r**	**i**	**t**	**e**	g	h	j	k	p

11e Wordmuddle

a-e	**cage**	**palace**	**private**
i-e	**beside**	**notice**	**admire**

ANSWERS (pages 24-25)

12. Magic 'e' 1
     'a-e', 'i-e'

Spelling Made Easy
Level 2 Textbook
Pages 32 - 35

12b Reading Comprehension

Correct answers should include the following key words.

1. **Fire**
2. **Pavement**
3. **Electric wire**
4. **Table**
5. **Damage**
6. **Basement**

12d Crossword

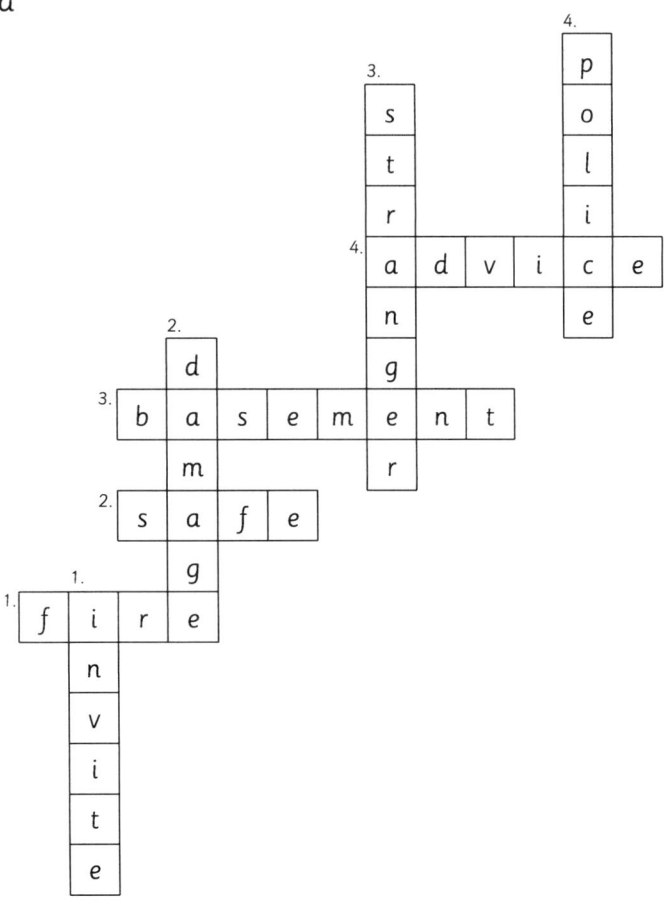

12e Wordsorting

a-e	**strange**	**disgrace**	**wages**
i-e	**tide**	**practice**	**nineteen**

ANSWERS (pages 26-27)

13. Magic 'e' 2
'o-e', 'u-e'

Spelling Made Easy
Level 2 Textbook
Pages 36 - 39

13b Reading Comprehension

Correct answers should include the following key words.

1. **Smoke**
2. **Clothes**
3. **Sure**
4. **Argue**
5. **Phone**
6. **Picture**

13c Pictures

hotel   **picture**   **phone**

13d Wordsearch

a	m	u	s	e	g	s	e	l	h
x	c	a	p	t	u	r	e	m	o
d	t	h	s	r	z	w	c	k	p
t	f	u	t	u	r	e	h	j	e
z	u	v	f	s	e	k	o	z	l
q	m	w	f	e	s	u	k	n	e
o	e	v	s	p	g	d	e	x	s
f	s	d	p	h	o	n	e	p	s
t	y	x	d	a	v	d	e	m	w
h	o	m	e	l	e	s	s	g	d

13e Wordmuddle

o-e	**hopeless**	**alone**	**explode**
u-e	**excuse**	**sure**	**clue**

ANSWERS (pages 28-29)

14. Magic 'e' 2
    'o-e', 'u-e'

Spelling Made Easy
Level 2 Textbook
Pages 36 - 39

14b Reading Comprehension

Correct answers should include the following key words.

1. **Phone**
2. **Potatoes/tomatoes**
3. **Injured**
4. **Close**
5. **Hopes**

14c Pictures

    tomatoes   **phone**   **picture**

14d Crossword

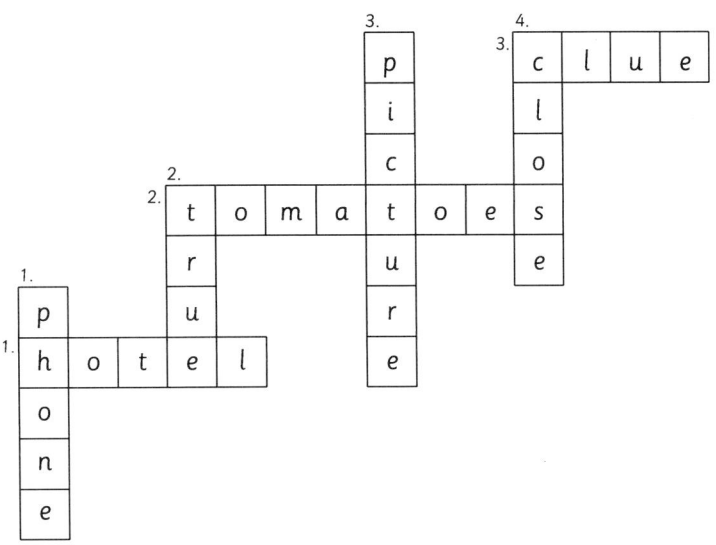

14e Wordsorting

o-e	**whole**	**rode**	**choking**
u-e	**refuse**	**cure**	**continue**

67

ANSWERS (pages 30-31)

15. Vowel Blending
'ai', 'oa', 'ir'

Spelling Made Easy
Level 2 Textbook
Pages 40 - 45

15b Reading Comprehension

Correct answers should include the following key words.

1. **Complain**
2. **Throat**
3. **Thirteen**
4. **Pain**
5. **Firmly**
6. **Cupboard**

15c Pictures

The **girl** moans and **groans**.

She has a **pain** in her leg.

Cherry holds the girl **firmly** by the waist.

Cherry goes to the **cupboard** to get a plaster.

15d Wordsearch

e	t	r	a	i	n	i	n	g	z
t	h	i	r	t	e	e	n	j	k
f	w	e	v	s	g	w	v	s	u
g	b	x	g	r	w	h	m	o	n
i	c	p	a	i	n	m	o	u	a
r	y	l	w	q	c	b	a	u	f
l	z	a	f	t	s	e	n	h	r
m	f	i	r	s	t	a	i	d	a
w	e	n	f	g	s	v	y	l	i
f	g	s	q	u	i	r	m	s	d

15e Wordmuddle

ai	**complain**	**snail**
oa	**throat**	**roar**
ir	**circus**	**girl**

ANSWERS (pages 32-33)

16. Vowel Blending
'ai', 'oa', 'ir'

Spelling Made Easy
Level 2 Textbook
Pages 40 - 45

16b Reading Comprehension

Correct answers should include the following key words.

1. **Cloakroom**
2. **Overcoat/raincoat/dufflecoat**
3. **Rail**
4. **Waiting**
5. **Firm**
6. **Twirls**

16d Crossword

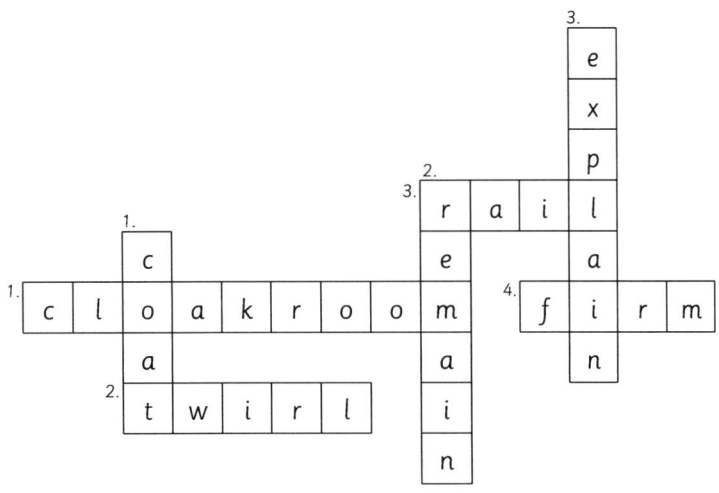

16e Wordsorting

ai	**main**	**trail**
oa	**float**	**oar**
ir	**circuit**	**first**

ANSWERS (pages 34-35)

17. Vowel Blending
'ou', 'ea', 'ur'

Spelling Made Easy
Level 2 Textbook
Pages 46 - 51

17b Reading Comprehension

Correct answers should include the following key words.

1. **Burglar**
2. **Surprised**
3. **Fountain**
4. **Thousand**
5. **Easy**

17c Pictures

curtains **ear** **fountain**

17d Wordsearch

a	d	s	**s**	**o**	**u**	**n**	**d**	p	e
m	w	**a**	**c**	**c**	**o**	**u**	**n**	**t**	**a**
o	q	v	c	s	g	h	x	m	**s**
u	z	x	s	a	r	j	**e**	k	**i**
n	f	**b**	**u**	**r**	**n**	**t**	**a**	m	**l**
t	q	r	o	s	g	y	**r**	p	**y**
e	t	f	h	l	v	x	c	n	m
f	**u**	**r**	**n**	**i**	**t**	**u**	**r**	**e**	u
g	y	d	c	s	**j**	**e**	**a**	**n**	**s**
p	w	**d**	**i**	**s**	**t**	**u**	**r**	**b**	**s**

17e Wordmuddle

ou	**sound**	**hour**
ea	**jeans**	**seasons**
ur	**disturb**	**pursue**

ANSWERS (pages 36-37)

18. Vowel Blending
   'ou', 'ea', 'ur'

Spelling Made Easy
Level 2 Textbook
Pages 46 - 51

18b Reading Comprehension

Correct answers should include the following key words.

1. **Murmur**
2. **Weary**
3. **Pleased**
4. **Outside**
5. **Curl up and sleep**
5. **Thousand pounds**

18c Picture

    leaves   **curtains**   **thousand**

18d Crossword

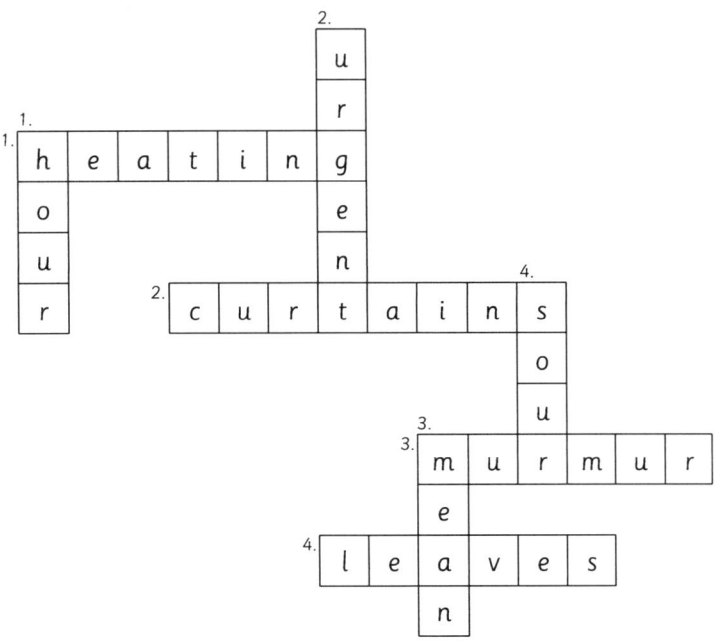

18e Wordsorting

ou	**lounge**	**flour**
ea	**leaning**	**gear**
ur	**turban**	**surname**

ANSWERS (pages 38-39)

19. Vowel Blending
'aw', 'oi', 'er'

Spelling Made Easy
Level 2 Textbook
Pages 52 - 57

19b Reading Comprehension

Correct answers should include the following key words.

1. **Strawberry**
2. **Nervous**
3. **Awful**
4. **Groceries**
5. **Choir**
6. **Foil**

19c Pictures

There has been a frost, but it has **thawed**.

Gus wraps the **leftover** food in kitchen **foil**.

Cherry gets groceries from the **supermarket**.

Gus sits down to do some more **drawing**.

19d Wordsearch

u	n	a	v	o	i	d	a	b	l	e
d	f	w	g	h	r	w	x	o	w	x
b	n	**f**	e	r	a	b	x	u	r	**c**
v	t	**u**	**j**	**o**	**i**	**n**	**e**	**d**	k	**e**
l	o	**l**	c	s	g	y	c	g	s	**r**
a	t	y	z	w	j	k	**h**	o	l	**t**
w	g	h	d	x	e	t	**o**	k	x	**a**
y	**g**	**r**	**o**	**c**	**e**	**r**	**i**	**e**	**s**	**i**
e	h	t	j	k	h	o	r	p	s	**n**
r	a	**d**	**r**	**a**	**w**	**i**	**n**	**g**	n	d
a	**n**	**e**	**r**	**v**	**o**	**u**	**s**	u	i	s

19e Wordmuddle

	aw	**jaw**	**thawed**
	oi	**choir**	**poison**
	er	**exercise**	**certain**

ANSWERS (pages 40-41)

20. **Vowel Blending**
'aw', 'oi', 'er'

Spelling Made Easy
Level 2 Textbook
Pages 52 - 57

20b Reading Comprehension

Correct answers should include the following key words.

1. **Drawing**
2. **Pointless**
3. **Interesting**
4. **Ointment**
5. **Understands**
6. **Bawling**

20d Crossword

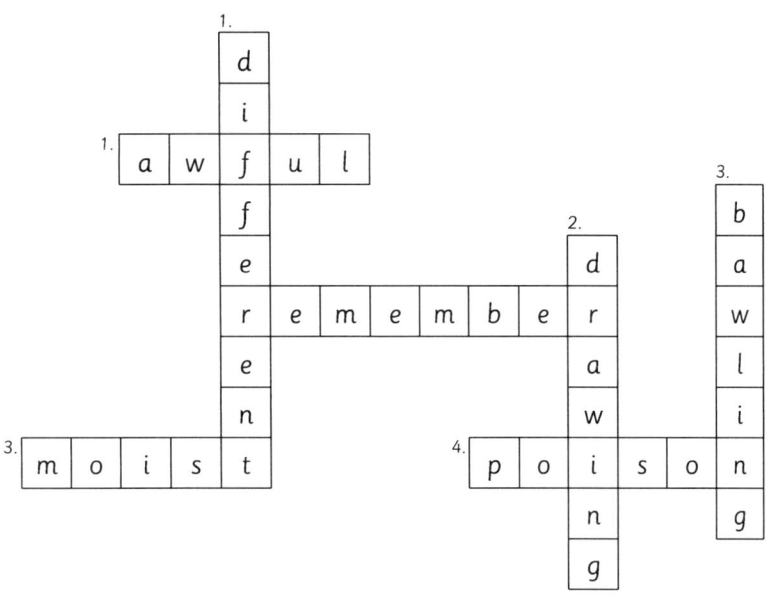

20e Wordsorting

aw	**prawn**	**sprawl**
oi	**oil**	**voice**
er	**spider**	**Germany**

ANSWERS (pages 42-43)

21. Vowel Blending
'al', 'ea' (short e), 'ow'

Spelling Made Easy
Level 2 Textbook
Pages 58 - 63

21b Reading Comprehension

Correct answers should include the following key words.

1. **Gradually**
2. **Drowsy**
3. **Feather**
4. **Towel**
5. **Rowdy**
6. **Stealthily**

21c Pictures

shower   **feather**   **hospital**

21d Wordsearch

d	f	**h**	**o**	**s**	**p**	**i**	**t**	**a**	**l**	j	**h**
r	o	v	w	**h**	q	a	c	b	t	s	**e**
m	c	r	h	**o**	h	**d**	**o**	**w**	**n**	w	**a**
t	f	g	s	**w**	j	k	l	t	y	c	**l**
h	w	q	c	**e**	z	g	r	h	j	**s**	**t**
r	e	u	i	**r**	v	x	e	b	m	**w**	**h**
e	**p**	**o**	**w**	**e**	**r**	**f**	**u**	**l**	x	**e**	**y**
a	a	d	s	f	b	t	s	e	g	**a**	m
t	b	g	h	d	e	s	w	t	p	**t**	u
e	d	**a**	**l**	**m**	**i**	**g**	**h**	**t**	**y**	**y**	w
n	q	c	f	a	g	r	x	h	j	f	s
s	t	**g**	**r**	**a**	**d**	**u**	**a**	**l**	**l**	**y**	u

21e Wordmuddle

al	**almighty**	**musical**
ea	**treasure**	**threatens**
ow	**allow**	**towel**

ANSWERS (pages 44-45)

22. Vowel Blending
'al', 'ea' (short e), 'ow'

Spelling Made Easy
Level 2 Textbook
Pages 58 - 63

22b Reading Comprehension

Correct answers should include the following key words.

1. **Washing-powder**
2. **Healthy, wealthy**
3. **Power point**
4. **Weather**
5. **Musical**

22c Picture

    power point   **wealthy**   **washing powder**

22d Crossword

```
              2.
              h
      1.
      p o w d e r
              a
  2.          l
  m u s i c a l
              t
              h
  3. 1.
  n a t u r a l l y
    l
    l      3.
    o      w
  4.
  w e a t h e r
  e        a
  d        l
           t
           h
           y
```

22e Wordsorting

al	**criminal**	**annually**
ea	**leather**	**ahead**
ow	**vowel**	**tower**

ANSWERS (pages 46-47)

23. Silent letters, a (ar) and Endings

Spelling Made Easy
Level 2 Textbook
Pages 64 - 69

23b Reading Comprehension

Correct answers should include the following key words.

1. **Beautifully**
2. **Wrote**
3. **Powerful**
4. **Aunty and uncle**
5. **Raspberries and sweet biscuits**

23c Pictures

It is almost as if they are in a **trance**.

Suddenly the phone rings.

Gus is a really talented **guy**!

Cherry fetches some **raspberries** and **sweet biscuits**.

23d Wordsearch

f	l	i	s	t	e	n	x	n	p
a	n	s	w	e	r	e	d	l	o
q	w	c	g	s	h	g	j	k	s
f	o	c	b	k	n	o	w	o	s
a	z	a	d	f	t	s	b	g	i
m	h	l	w	r	o	t	e	u	b
i	u	m	c	k	s	l	m	y	l
l	i	u	a	u	n	t	y	n	e
y	t	y	x	s	b	g	s	u	o
b	t	h	a	n	k	f	u	l	w

23e Wordmuddle

Silent Letter	**soften**	**biscuit**
a	**passport**	**calm**
Ending	**sensibly**	**powerful**

ANSWERS (pages 48-49)

24. Silent letters, a (ar) and Endings

Spelling Made Easy
Level 2 Textbook
Pages 64 - 69

24b Reading Comprehension

Correct answers should include the following key words.

1. **Guests**
2. **Often**
3. **Knot**
4. **Wonderful**
5. **Fasten**

24d Crossword

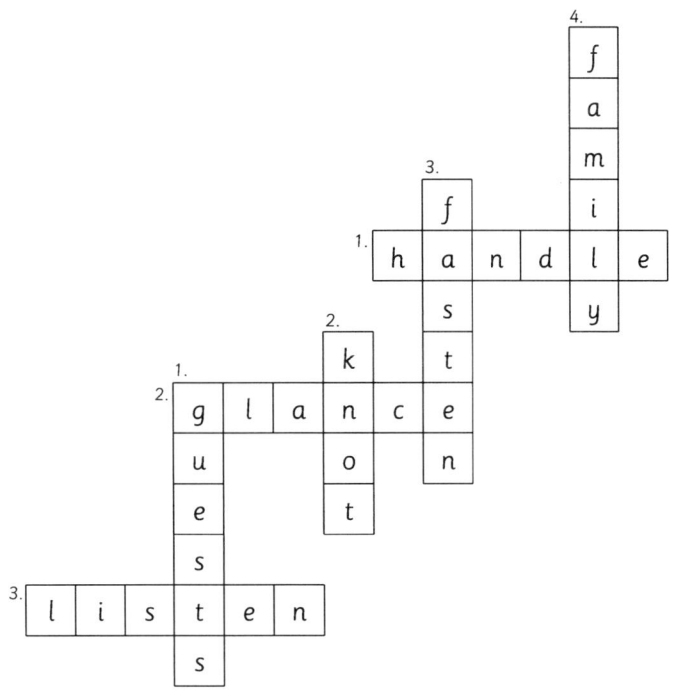

24e Wordsorting

Silent Letter	**tongue**	**honest**
a	**France**	**calf**
Ending	**simple**	**horribly**

ANSWERS (pages 50-51)

25. Various

Spelling Made Easy
Level 2 Textbook
Pages 70 - 75

25b Reading Comprehension

Correct answers should include the following key words.

1. **Discussion**
2. **Nervous**
3. **Obey, request**
4. **Laugh**
5. **Not his fault**
6. **Ridiculous**

25c Pictures

      nervous   **laugh**   **serious**

25d Wordsearch

a	c	**n**	**o**	**w**	**h**	**e**	**r**	**e**	x
w	**n**	**a**	**u**	**g**	**h**	**t**	**y**	y	n
o	d	s	a	c	v	b	a	u	t
g	h	o	d	j	k	u	g	f	c
r	**i**	**d**	**i**	**c**	**u**	**l**	**o**	**u**	**s**
w	t	**f**	e	v	b	s	g	t	j
u	**o**	**a**	v	**p**	**o**	**l**	**i**	**t**	**e**
x	**b**	**u**	z	c	g	d	y	u	o
p	**e**	**l**	o	**s**	**i**	**l**	**e**	**n**	**t**
m	**y**	t	s	**e**	**r**	**i**	**o**	**u**	**s**

25e Wordmuddle

    au   **author**   -ous   **jealous**
    -ious   **envious**   -sion   **discussion**
    i   **iron**   -o   **obey**

ANSWERS (pages 52-53)

26. **Various**

Spelling Made Easy
Level 2 Textbook
Pages 70 - 75

26b Reading Comprehension

Correct answers should include the following key words.

1. **Bicycle**
2. **Australia**
3. **Delicious**
4. **Sausages and cauliflower and cheese sauce**
5. **Motor-bike**
5. **Precious**

26c Picture

sausages　　　**motor-bike**　　　**bicycle**

26d Crossword

								c	
	s							u	
	a				n	o	t	i	c	e
	u							o	
	c							u	
e	x	c	u	r	s	i	o	n	s
	a								
	u								
	l								
b	i	c	y	c	l	e			
	f								
	l								
	o								
	w								
p	r	e	c	i	o	u	s		
	r								

26e Wordsorting

au	**taught**	-ous	**tremendous**
-ious	**anxious**	-sion	**admission**
i	**diamond**	-o	**ghost**